FIELD THEORIES

FIELD THEORIES
SAMIYA BASHIR

Nightboat Books
New York

ISBN: 978-1-937658-63-2

Design and typesetting by HR Hegnauer
Text set in Perpetua and Calibri

Cover art by Toyin Ojih Odutola, *Lonely Chambers (T.O.)*, 2011
© Toyin Ojih Odutola. Courtesy of the artist and Jack Shainman Gallery, New York

Author photo by Kenan Banks

Cataloging-in-publication data is available from the Library of Congress

Distributed by University Press of New England
One Court Street
Lebanon, NH 03766
www.upne.com

Nightboat Books
New York
www.nightboat.org

To my Pops

waan ku jeclahay aabe

$$I(\nu,T) = \frac{2h\nu^3}{c^2} \cdot \frac{1}{e^{h\nu/kT} - 1}$$

one full Black lily
luminescent
in a homemade field

June Jordan

Consequences of the laws of thermodynamics

When Albert Murray said
the second law adds up to
the blues that in other words
ain't nothing nothing he meant it

not quite the way my pops says
nomads don't show emotions
but more how my grandmother
warned that men like women

with soft hands blood red
nails like how Mingus meant
truth if you had time for it
facts if you got no time that

years pass. Zero
one two three and
the man you used

to flirt with you
no longer flirt with
thank goodness.

He's now a man
you can't wear
your jaw out on

about weather
news or work

a perfect
strawberry

buried
beneath

a peck.

Paleontology

I step from the airplane. My hair melts dead air. I walk quickly: click-clunk, click-clunk, click-clunk. Barbara Jordan, bronze and sober, glasses poised, the last me I'll see for three more days and three more days forever. Outside I slow the click-clunk to a three-sound crawl: click-clickclunk &etc. I am a woolly mammoth waiting at the cab stand. I am a woolly mammoth stuffed into a cab. I bear the long silence of my own extinction through the rear view. My head on the back seat: horns akimbo: I melt dead air. Blame humans for the loss of large mammals like myself, a new study suggests. My cousin tuktuks my husk to a dry diorama. The radio blares: "The tide is high." The radio sings: "I'm gonna be your number one."

Synchronous rotation

After Dizzy rolled Bags Jackson
and his vibes outta Detroit

Bags wrote his love songs in
the minor keys. Said the minor

registers the heart. The magnet
of us: iron filings thrown up

the greedy gullet of space
before one turn humbles

another slow as hours plucked
through catgut blue. Please,

the old song goes, send me
someone to love. Me? Who

am I kidding? Every day I meet
some minor love or two.

Hey you:

let's toss our tarantellas
across the tracks. Let's

reveal one another
bit by puckered bit. Let's

emit this fit of heat
before we burn.

Or let's burn.

Notions of temperature

bold as gonzo bumming our smokes two grackles top an aspen branch

      again : again

to suffer

      from the vulgar latin original meaning undergo meaning endure

fulcanelli

      cold-hearted fuck

transmogrify

      this bastard luck

cassini-huygens

      we need some tit-

      ian water for our thirst

to suffer

      compare old french sofrir meaning accept

      meaning tolerate meaning breathless meaning

breathless our grackles drip ash : drip

      feed them our yew trees someone says

      swat them their flies someone won't stop saysing

Blackbody curve

Stairs: a rushed flight down thirty-eight; French doors unlocked always.

Always: a lie; an argument.

Argument: two buck hunters circle a meadow's edge.

Edge: one of us outside bleeding.

Bleeding: shards of glass; doors locked.

Locked: carpet awash with blood.

Blood: lift and drop; a sudden breeze.

Breeze: its whistle though bone.

Bone: the other was looking at —

Bone: cradled to catch drips.

Drips: quiet as a meadow fawn.

Fawn: faces down each hunter each gun.

Gun: again.

Again: somebody call someone.

Someone: almost always prefers forgetting.

Forgetting: an argument; a lie.

Lie: a meadow; a casement; a stair.

Planck's constant

What else made sense but
the push to climb one another

hand over hand and grab at
whoever was near enough?

The season groaned on
into November; crows bled

branch to sky; stone upon
stone upon stone towered

toward a heaven that flushed
its three-day-old lie of bruise.

Snowflakes threatened war
the moon split town and swore

not to return for days. Your
flicker and turn a lighthouse

and a storm. At quarter to six
the sun went down forever so

what else made sense but to
climb one another hand over

hand and cleave to whoever was
left and near enough and would?

Ground state

bend into my mouth
before frost ends us

this long year
I've lumbered — spin
devour spin — paced this crest

impatient for your nest
to tumble my nest for

the hum of your dulcet strum
and when I must bear you — maw

each strand still between my teeth
bend into my mouth

impatient for the tumble
I'll weave of you the dust
of a thousand more of us

lace the absence of your touch
into a clutch

Transitive relations

Her 'fro had gone lumpy at the left. They hadn't been themselves for ages. Yes:

She queried but they could only grunt a bit croak a bit. Their eyes locked in hazes. Yes:

She chose to love. She chose to make some pie. Yes:

She gathered kindling gathered rubes hung swollen from disuse. Yes:

She knew a sly sass who pointed out which branches birthed best. Yes:

She decided to love. She decided to make pomaceous pie. Yes:

She knelt to her oven. Smoke filled her right then left eye. Yes:

She sat back and rocked knee to heel. She stirred and she stirred and — Yes.

General relativities

Just then I met a man who wore a dead
woman's wedding band to every first date.
Who bought a round of drinks. Maybe
two. People struggle, Russ says, before he
does the bird: one leg kicked up, both
wings flapping. When my body gets too
solid I can ghost invisibler and invisibler.
Even then, almost clear, my knees still
hurt. I did that. Me. My upstage left part
— there — rumbles a cumulonimbus snee-

Carnot cycle

Only sometimes does homegrown bedrock glow moneygreen.
Sometimes rock whines mommy. Sometimes rock coos baby.
Sometimes rock calls late with the mortgage. Sometimes rock
knits shoulder blades right where you can't pluck.

Early mornings something doesn't sit right over the sink. Sits crooked.
Slumps askew. Body doesn't lay the way you left it. Squinting
gets you nowhere. You squat to the floor and feel around. Stop.
Smell for it. Shrug. Still some dangling something modifies you.
Smackdab midchest you feel lumpy empty. Sniff. Sniff.

Shrug.

Days. Almost every one we grab pickaxes. Almost every one we mine.
We hum worksongs. We sing hymns. We chip worry stone. We
hope. We gather moss. We lie flat. We scratch at the mineshaft.
We descend deeper. We lamp away from the light not toward
exit but through the broken core.

Universe as an infant: fatter than expected and kind of lumpy

I sit on a white sofa and talk with Groucho
Marx. We both move in and through
character. I sit a bit intimidated. Groucho says
to me, pulling his cigar from his mouth, he
says, I sent you an email. He nods his white
phone to the white phone somehow in my
pocket. I gotta go to the crapper, he says. I'll
be right back, he says all no-words and cigar-
points. Alone I check my phone. His email
simple: blahblahblah Einstein blahblahblah
theory. He returns drained and we lay into
our couch corners like two old lovers reading
the Sunday Times. We blow smoke rings and
shape them into big beaned cloud gates with
our minds. Scientists in LA just discovered
that elephants run like you do, I tell him. He
mimes punching me in the face. Then laughs.

Now we're on the vaudeville stage. People
outside wear straw hats, sell caramel apples
and kettle corn confections. Trolleys skate the
streets. The old theater fills to rafters and we
do our bits do our sketches. I do my elephant
bit where I ride my bicycle around and around
and Groucho is on foot giving slapstick chase.
People ride onstage from their seats. Elephant
people like me. A bicycle conga-line.

Then it's all post-show stuff. Audiences want so much. I'll find myself outside and jump on a bus. A Blue Bird. First I'll buy some kettle corn muffins. When my bus comes I'll run to catch it, hang on through the pull-away streetcar-style. I'll pay the driver an astonishing sum. I can't be sure, but he'll promise I'm on the right bus, that I should step back behind the black leather line. And I will. And I'll sit. I'll eat my kettle corn muffin. Again, I'll finger the white phone that somehow buzzes my pocket. Again, I'll show myself in.

We must know a force
greater than our weaknesses.

Jean Toomer

Third law

each september we suck coffee down like arsenic

tony vanishes through the annex bowel   again

chain split vowels give me away like television

each café blazes to approximate ash

teevees rush the streets on their own two feet

air pockets meet hush meet crush meet moan

we eat our phones

Methods of heat transfer

hooyo's healing foot holds the open front door

rugs unroll beneath keening rows

dusk lazes miles down the road

everyone is starved

a child leans into reality somewhere

another swears about lost controls

— bismillahi —

can i borrow the car

moonshine balances a scalding plate out of reach

one after another enters kissing kissing kissing

heavy lids smack wet the outside winds

Grandma, why did you cut my long hair short?

When I say radiation I mean

light that you cannot contain

Your mother has enough worry without you.

Relations between planets and stars

— and the little girl caught three small fish with the rod her grandpa
made her

carried goose feathers in hand she'd found on the sand let grandma hold
the reel while she ran one way then back and showed off her prize and
decided her feathers were too big to fly a duck through the sky

— and the fish flopped on land once caught

grandma unhooked them threw them to earth one then another then
another and they flipped and jumped and gasped and jumped and flipped

— and the little girl wheeled and wheeled

called grandpa back to see what she'd created *look!* the little girl
wheeled *i caught them all!* and wheeled and grabbed grandma's bag
and wheeled and jumped like a linefish and jumped like a dockfish
[jumping] *look!* [jumping] *look!* [jumping] *look!*

Particle .˙. Wave

Pops bailed the basement with box-store towels with pots with pans. Kidfeet creaked up stairs to dump sop then tromped back down for more. Again. News: climate folks warn of these more frequent storms. My credit card's magnet was shot last year. I wanted to replace it. Really. The bank lived right up the road but I just couldn't. Things go awry and mostly I just let them. I worry. I wait for pops to slip in all that water, but he doesn't. And the kidfeet keep the march up. The descent. Return his flood to the bloated earth. Repeat.

Radio .˙. Wave

this cookie walked
her brown-hair
across the road

her bindlestick skillet
an easeful balance
of two dozen eggs

her pockets buzzed
her clothes bored
to black holes

the radio said
we'd soon leave
our rockets here

sail the starlight winds
start anew and again
promises

promises
in America
Eocene camels

roamed tinycute
would've made
such nice pets

my father and I
still blind from camel
spit — the excuse of it —

try ways to stop stopping
and going but this cookie
passes our stand and

for a minute or two
we're all of us just
damp desert nomads

if we'd mate our phone
with her phone she'd crack
her eggs and light us a fire

where we'd sit and stitch sails
toss our shells and miss Sirius
nip his master's bow

Dag! We ain't even in Detroit yet? Sheeeit.
Stop here and lemme get me some chicken.

— then two women one old and one young pulled aside
off the highway and into the poorly lit driveway of popeye's
off i-94 in a truck stop. they wanted to buy some fried chicken.
one had a five and the other three ones and together they purchased
a three piece two biscuits a leg and a thigh

                                          and they let
the poor girl with the pockmarked-up face and the torn
lace from panties caught up in her apron just
                                   keep the change.
so she did and she quietly squirreled away five

                                   for herself
and then later that night after steaming in dark lint-lined slacks
made of fake polyester and worn to a shine smelling french
fried and coated in salt stains the dusty bill rose it emerged
from that pockmarked girl's pocket and slid to the palm

of the man singing —
                     newport! five dollars! five dollars!
who kept it aloft in his palm where the wind swept the frail
greasy paper up into the air far above where the man waved
his smokes

far above far above where a mother was bent
out her window then down to the baby who leaned sorta
safely up next to its grates. it fell right on his hand
which was sticky with chef boyardee or spaghettios maybe
who cares. i mean really

who cares but the breeze
and the bill and the man selling smokes
because mama needs 'ports so that kid
— lucky kid — reaches up and gets lifted.

Sore broken in the place of dragons

how we pockmark our
sickening ball of melt:

how we crawl among animals
having forgotten their names:

how we swoon redfaced and coy
to our small silly star:

how we fall in love a little each
crisp stupid winter:

how we bow clavicles against
nights long and snowquiet:

how we can't recall midsummer
even in its midst:

how we cease awe at the jerk
of our cretinous work:

how we breathe out our parasitic breath then
breathe it in:

how we watch again as light breaches
our wobbly horizon:

how we know the time has arrived
to rise:

Blackbody radiation

witness = vulnerability

∴

take it

∴

crack whip

+

endure

∵

punishment enjoyed =

(breathe in.)

(breathe out.) + 1

∵

smoke stench ≤

secret

≤

what if you're running

·

what if you're running

·

what if you're running

∴

witness

Sometimes in a body

little metal insects tic   tic   tic   tic   tic   tic   tic   tic   tic

through bloodstreaks through musculoskeletal structure

sometimes a body sits by a window and watches an online party feed skipping
the party

sometimes a body makes itself sick when pushed too hard too long

says stop

shhhhhh

stop

the wonderful singer told us we were the black gold of the sun on repeat

why wonderful singer?

how much is black gold even worth?

sometimes a body finds drugs where it least expects them

holes have been dug and drugs buried into the holes

how light speed equals need equals constancy

how we small each other

how we bind each other

sometimes a body counts twelve stars where skies never blacken never clear

they look lonely

Manistee light

Brother I don't either understand
this skipscrapple world —

these slick bubble cars zip feverish
down rushes of notcorn of notbeets

notcabbage and the land and the land —

you should know, man, nothing
grows down here anymore except

walloped wishes and their gouged out
oil cans. Where notbloodroot spans us

guard towers land mine the sand.
They twist us. They tornado us. No —

Do spring breezes bring the scent of smelt?

Remember? Even on strike our mother
gathered smelt by their fingery bagfuls

and fried them whole. I wish I knew
how she did it. It was almost enough.

Law of total probability

hear the particular problem of chicken of egg of ir   .tion of life of
moving to manhattan with four dollars and an uptown surfer sofa
of industry temping or being in first after securi   ot thinkin' of
myself as either young or cute of others who did who were men who
were neither of the old guy on the security desk who thought my fear
no implac   terror of guns was cute   arable of his reminiscence
about guns not killing and people killing of the badge in his draw
from his force reti   ment, of how i cross the street away from cops of
my being black and all of his being black and all of him taking it out his
gun of its girth of its power of its bullets of 38 calibers of his age that
was older than 38 of my age that was so much younger of the gun that
was exactly that — a 38 built for force

and the bullets were huge — see and the safety was on — see and
nothing could be safe than a gun in good hand afety engaged nothing
to fear — see and when it went off its bullet ore through old guy's
security desk and whizzed past my hip so close it burned the breeze
and at 8am we were alone and when 38 holes blew through the office
door and through the elevator wall and through some industry ex
office who was still downtown eating his downtown breakfast and
cursing whatever negro artist he cursed that morning old y's job
was through and it's too bad and he was such a nice old g nd i'm
pretty sure i'm supposed to say that last part

You think I'll be the dark sky so you can be the star?
I'll swallow you whole.

Warsan Shire

CORONAGRAPHY

John Henry opens his mouth —

I can tell your future too — wan' hear it?
Most don't and fine by me ain't got nothing

but time now nohow. Hands been full since day
one: swinging. Swinging — *was I born with it?* —

the night I came shocked Mama and Daddy
to the corners of our old dark quarters

caul washed down to the floor where I tore it
threw it fists swinging and grasping for air.

When I said — *Mama?* she dropped me clear to
the floor and jumped back quick — *Mama I'm'a*

be — but she dropped her head in her hands and
cried — *Papa   I'm'a   be   steel* — I started

— *I'm'a die with my hammer my* — was I
born with it? — *Mama don't cry. I'm'a be* —

Polly Ann jumps her broom —

I swear I wasn't born to cry so I'd
be a lie if I say I wept when I
left my mama's house — like I ain't know life
up here would be hardscrabble rough — what's not?

And I loved the blue he grew from his eyes
and spread to the syrup-sap drip of his
dip-step. And I loved how he loved mine. And
how could I know he'd risk us — and for what?

For what? Why build us a life here just to
end it? I kept dry eyes — I swear — I stood
stronger than I looked. I stood fragile and
heavy as a honeybee. So did he.

A man's heart rocks like mine for the kinda
love — found and fed — that tells him he ain't dead.

John Henry's first real swing —

I stood hungry   near dead   and the man said
my hammer'd give us shelter   keep us fed.

That's what he said. But instead I was drove
up these craggy mountain roads. I was gave

another hammer and a crust of bread
and not-enough slop to anger my plate.

I ate what I could. I practiced on wood.
I split rocks as the nights stretched long. I chipped

blocks of ice when I couldn't sleep. Couldn't
keep — listen — whether it kills me later

or now I'm gone. I know how. I know why.
I got these forty pounds of fire-bolt the

color of sorrow smoked eyes that I lift
and drop. Lift and drop. Lift and drop. Lift and —

Polly Ann has an ordinary day —

Lift and drop. Lift and drop. This baby and
these bags of rags I wash day in day out
keep me on the useful side of madness.

Stout as he stands his tenderness caught me
cupped me his stooped kisses fixed my flutter.
Face it — all my time I spend picking up
putting down moving things around and still

I can't drown out the *whop whop whop* of steel
of big men fast women got their scent up
hot to how his hammer cuts quick the breeze

— I'm useful. I'm my milking body and
another slung around me like hard rock.
I'm dreaming us laced   us dropped so low it
sounds like shaking
                    feels like screams
                                    ain't neither.

John Henry feels fate —

Felt like shaking   sounded like screams   wasn't
nothing but hot air and hot noise coughing

up hillside coming bent over double-
jointed wheezing vapors and threats. He rode

a devil that whistled my name —
                              John — John —
that whispered of numbers and days —
                                    John — John —

he rumbled up in that high saddle seat
early on Friday morning waxing his

merchant smirk
                    he came to take us back down
off this mountain back —
                         I said I done been

where I been and ain't going again — with
my last breath I'd drill that devil to death —

I'd swing step or kick but before I'd die
I'd try anything quick —
                         metal! stone! stick!

Dark things have a way of manifesting themselves.

Neil deGrasse Tyson

Second law

Who was warned about these things:
the neverhush, the maddening chafe
sliding down a reddened bridge, print
disappearing   disappearing?

Who was told how to brook it?
The houndstooth stench of olding.
That time just runs itself out. That
we Sisyphus ourselves to glasses,
hobble wreckage down stair
after bricky stair.

That once we leave home — its gaseous
oven — that once we walk the same slow
steps as our hide-and-seek sun that
once we face our anti-lovers' anti-gaze:
bright, open, later, now eyes smoldered
coats swept open to flash our own
scarred bellies our own hot hands
ablaze with spent matches with burnt-out
love —

Remember love?

How it loosed its jaw to our kisses?
How it unhinged us? How it tried us

like so many keys like so many rusted
locks? How it missed its target despite its
kicking? How maybe its force could kill us?

Without it what's left day after day
to trundle our legs? What's left to push
breath ragged and torn from our lungs?

Who was warned
how these solar winds would leave us
brown and bruised as apples over-
-ripe host and blowsy   seed dis-
appearing   disappearing?

Were you?

Me too.

**You don't have to pump the breaks you just gotta
keep your eyes on the road**

You know how the universe blinks and we
exist for a minute or two with our

classic hits stations and our marshmallows
our wars and flags and television and

shit. Coke bottles falling from the sky to
an old man's village and the white people just

laugh and laugh and line up to pay and laugh
and get paid and laugh. That's what they made.

He'll clean it up. This is the world spinning
its circle in the vast dark and this is

us arguing the same shit on a new
machine. Faster. The world stays unstable

anyway. We work all day to excess
and for what? What will we make of it? Try

to recall the red crest of a robin's
breast in springtime. Springtime! When we fight our

machines with our machines through our machines.
It's the thought that hurts. When we stand one hand

airborne one finger on play. When we pump
the volume up against the god damned bird

song. Anyway. *She even got a breast*
reduction, my friend said, *that's how stupid*

she is, my friend said. An anthropocene
of wannabe hepcats wanting to be.

But this is the world spinning in the vast
dark. Not any of the million spots we

see in the night sky but the one we
can't. Rushing to the serenity shop

and fighting and hiding and crying and
eating in our cars with our volume pumped

against the birdsong. We are animals.
We need orgasm regularly. Now

even that lies just out of reach hostage
to the ding of our nearby cells — a poke

a text a like a love a comment: WELL
DONE! Aaaahhh! Aaaaahhh! Aaaahhh. Aaahhh. Aaahh. Aaah. Aah. Ah. a.

Yearn for the road. Ache for the unfettered
journey. Grow weary of it. Namaste

the mat says. Killed people kill people it
says. Shock. Disbelief. Wildly darting eyes.

Same old jive. Look steady through the pane.
Go on. Trust me. Really take in the light.

Upon such rocks

A body. A zoo. A lovely savannah. Walls of clear, clean glass. Fresh food when they feed it. When it doesn't pace impatience and fend for its own fool self. It's a fool. There's a door. Door after door after door. Glossy paws shaped for knob turning. Every door leads to a new savannah. Each savannah bumps new clean glass. Light cyclopses a never-ending tap tap tap tap loud on good weather days. Tap tap tap tap two by four two by four can't get through the door. Tap tap tap through a trellised stream. Break. No.

Positions of the body that force it to touch its own flesh. Positions that don't. Hallelujah. Chairs turned backward. Straddled so legs can spread can breathe so arms can lift can rest can fold can lean. Bless the burying of chins into a crook. Bless standing. Bless rest. Don't be afraid. Don't be afraid. Don't be afraid. Keep going.

A body won't always put mind or heart before lips or eyes before feet. Needs me to keep it from falling face down in the road. Can't breathe without some salve to moisten the air. Me neither. Needs water to stop its eyes crying blood. Can't account for how it returns or as whom or as what but knows how to coax a languid kundalini toward dewpoint. Knows it is little more than slush-slop water. Knows not seventy percent but through and through. Heard somewhere only birdbrains test water's depth with both feet. Well, hell, I whisper. Keep going.

If it were a preacher a body'd lean on its pulpit, pound its fists like emphasis to block out the pain. Where does its pain sit right now? Knees? Ankles? Hips? Shoulders holding the whole thing up against pulpit? Keep going.

It's tall but likes high heels. It remembers wearing short skirts and high shoes. Can it tell you why it stopped? Maybe it'll whisper it. Maybe it'll just tell me. I'll tell it I'll keep it's secret. I'll lie. Keep going.

Right. Pain. A body can sprain ankles so much they no longer trust it. Without ankles a body falls and busts up its knee. Again. For a while there it sprains everything over and over. It is a glutton for punishment. It punishes and punishes and punishes and punishes and — don't be afraid —

cries about it. Not to anyone who'd listen. No one listens until it stops falling upon, and just becomes, cement. Until it ceases to come forward at finger becks, at calls. Two by four! Two by four! Once it woke from nightmares screaming balloons! screaming rainbows! and squished its sandblown eyes still as death with a humbird heart. When they feed it fresh meat against the glass it sleeps again. Don't be afraid. It sits. Don't be afraid. It eats. Don't be afraid. It thinks. Be a little afraid. Keep going.

We call it dark matter because it doesn't interact with light

Let this notice serve as replacement

    : the Department of State warns

        of the dangers of travel to   to

to   to   to   to   to

    . We recommend that citizens avoid all

travel to   to   to   to   to

whatever we've left for   . Everything east of

Moscow is a joke. Moscow is a joke. Leave

    out of your   . Ask yourself why

   you want to go to   ? Those niggers are

crazy. Understand: nothing you need exists

between   and   . We

protect   widespread banditry. Terrorist

operatives have demonstrated their intent to

attack   . Intermittently these notices

apply in the domestic sphere. When you   ,

don't say we didn't warn you.

Perform since you must perform

The old carriage house looks older
and its people and its dogwoods

scream across night-weary sight.
A widow drives her joystick chair

through early equinox light in
quiet Burlington. Blind, arthritic

in a full slip, she insists
her bra be worn the way

she's always worn her bra
her pleats lay the way

she lays her pleats. Knuckled
knots steer her toward another

vinyl back slick already from
sleepless footprints. Her daughter

who year after year saves Satyricon
for its cold gray end whispers:

imagine. Whispers: imagine a goddess
a charioteer propelling our minor gods.

Field theories

sold for poker chips
left cold left thawed left

bent into the yawp
ass up

let be
let air

bones
unknowns

ash
everywhere

curved space
dark — breath

dark — breath
dark — what?

sold for bluff on blind
left choked

left down
left bent

left passed
catch

How a body grabs a body.
Hungry. Even Jesus let

his bakers dozen fend
for themselves once

they got to snipping and
sipping too comfortably.

According to the literature.
Jesus. That first bite.

Its sharp. Its ache.
Its nectar. We'll

build a fort and fill it
with maple trees gone gaudy

with cobalt wishing stones.
We'll crawl inside and imagine

how maybe we used to laugh.
Fuck Orpheus and fuck them

for loving him for not loving who
we love when we're the ones

down here rotting in hell.
Huh? Music?

Anyone ever really heard us sing?
Let's move this: anyone ever asked?

Even so we sing all day. Even so we pass
our hours whatever ways we can —

We know some folk don't listen.
Just look. And trace. Look:

What is a thing of beauty
if not us?

Bear where a clothespin clips a nose
and breath is held until —

Bear it then keep walking
toward light. Right? Wait —

We'll ask them to name something
blue and maybe they'll say:

popsicle tongue
broken finger

black eye. Easy enough
to say *You*. Don't.

What does anyone out here know
of us? How

our tar-stained wings hide
what ergot saddles we ride. How

between our teeth we mash
the fur of maritime beasts. Still

some folk never thanks us
to manifest their pleas. Yet

what is a thing of beauty
if not us? Repeat:

dark — breath
dark — breath

dark — things we do as
we turn slowly blue:

lead laser dots through another
chalk outline; pick up today's

halloween dress; cry
at commercials; obey; pay

defense department rates
for a sandwich; unremember

memorable jingles; jaw
sandwiches that taste just like

sandwiches; figure we can't
expect much more than that; don't.

Some slaves only get free enough
to crouch in Kentucky foxholes

with Cincinnati just over
one last swift river.

Our own acrid smell finally
wakes us. Eras. Halfwoke

slowroll through the wet spot.
Panic. Floor. Hard. Years.

The worst kiddie-porn
we'll never say we see.

Bottles. Cans. Pizza box
hotels. Crusty burrito

bits. Razor blades.
Mirror shards. Cat puke.

Half a joint. Shuffled match.
Broken brick. Bloody steps.

Lit joint. Burnt fingers. Better.
Wash the hair/don't wash the hair.

Wash the hair/don't wash the hair.
Wash the hair/don't wash the hair.

Own no time. Late as fuck. Strip
the bed. Consider the stain. Don't.

The murk we blow to cool.
The slop and bang we curse.

The hum of incandescence.
The lip burns we nurse.

The best skin of our lives.
The best skins of our lives.

What is a thing of beauty
if not us?

Repeat:

Ha ha ha niggers are the worst

you know like how she would lie down in
her dark cornered room with an old movie
and remember again just how normal just
everyday just cold just buck wild casual just
sidewalk crack each smack in the face was just
every day buried in every part of speech just
life and she was just all in it you too you'd just
go ha ha ha niggers are the worst remember
and not even stop to think about why her
stomach hurt how come she had all that pain
in her side or the side of her head why she
needs new glasses just ha ha ha niggers are
the worst and sometimes she stood big as a
house and sometimes she was the house and
her neighbors wished she'd keep her blinds
closed please wished she'd pick up and move
please but there's so much to lift so much to
move   what she's not allowed to say   i'm
lonely   what she's not allowed to say   this
is hard   what she's not allowed to say
i wish someone would hold me would let me
hold them for just one full minute   what
she's not allowed to do   cry where we can
see her   and laugh ha ha ha   ha ha ha   ha
ha ha niggers are the worst   remember?   ha
ha ha   ha ha ha   ha ha ha   ha ha ha nig-

Are you sure, sweetheart, that you want to be well?

Toni Cade Bambara

CORONAGRAPHY

Polly Ann fears her future —

Where I fare 'tween metal stone and stick quick
wages quick drinks quick talk quick death quick saves
fast friendships laying quick odds to fast ends —

where I fare I can't no longer tell. Comes
a time when the look in a man's eyes says

you ain't there — nowhere — says he's thinking of
action and you steel your mind and think where

you left your get-busy shoes. Anything
you ask is answered by movement and rush

so you move you rush you wonder all day
if the cook looks nasty or the food don't

taste clean all the sudden does climbing hill
full of my corn-and-collard sweetness not —

— *well*
      well —

             what about what I was meant for?

John Henry tests his hammer's weight —

What about what I was meant for — *swinging* —
her   me   our son   our carpetbag home   was

I — *swinging* — meant to live and work and fear
nothing on cold nights we hold up huddled

beneath her mama's wedding quilt getting
warm? What about it? I tried to tell her

steel don't own me — you do I'd say *I'm glad*
to do anything   anything   but please

don't ask me this.
                    Takes more than heart to make
a man and these here hands — and hers — were all

I'd want or need.
                  Hammer and speed lead me
so high I smell sea above the treetops
— *swinging* — but all I drill don't mean nil if
I can't share it   have to bear it alone.

Polly Ann cuts quick the breeze —

Wasn't nothing but to bear it — let 'em
alone and act grown. Every day threats swirl
all up and down this hill   all dervish to
swish my steps and scuffle me to the side

like what's me and mine ain't mine. Pies and cakes
mount the tunnel's mouth   the same old sugar
cane siren songs with fresh lemonade with
sweet tea with cherry wine   swig for a swirl.

He stays too caught in his up and swing to
taste that talcum swimming through shale dust to

dot his lips and steal a kiss with every
lift. But — busy as I am — I notice

every rose-water eddy. I see each
germ blow past me like I'm not even there.

John Henry stakes his claim —

This germ blew past like we weren't standing there
him riding his machine like Orion

coming for our throats. We dug this. Every
spot was once our hands on rock. He come to

take what we built and we ain't gon' let him
not me not my shakers not this mountain

we peeled not none of us. He blew past us
coughing hot air hot noise like he don't know

who opened up this mouth — *Lord* — *Lord* — we ain't
gon' let him take it. Not food from our mouths.

Not what we make what we push through hand to
mouth and keep pushing. Not everything. All

he wants is all we have.
                                    If we let him
choke his way to it then who are we?
                                                        Who?

Polly Ann claims her stake —

Who we gonna be? We can choke or bust
this yoke. Who we gonna be? Preacher said

we rode that train together. We promised
we'd stay that way too but that don't mean don't

move when time comes for us to move to stretch
ourselves around each other — *Lord* — *Lord* — and

just leave here. But say I say *let's go let's*
lift up make life new say I knew I smelled

danger and said so too he'd ask *where would*
we go? what would we do? 'Swhen I knew I'd

do whatever it was I could to blaze
around or through that haze he caught — get taught

to swing that hammer if I had to though
everyone up here called me crazy — *mmph* —

I always knew I'd go to space.

Mae Jemison

First law

Sky threatens greensky storm.

Teevee says: You are *not* the father!

Cross the highway in the rain.

Stand between the highway rain.

Drip olive. Drip blue. Drip to work:

My bank! My bank of tellers askance!

Throw arms wide and spin and spin and spin.

Spin faster. Dizzy. Faster. Dizzy. Faster. Dizzy —

You are *not* the father *not* the father!
You are *not* the father *not* the father!
You are *not* the father *not* the father!
You are *not* the father *not* the father!

You are *not* the father *not* the father!
You are *not* the father *not* the father!
You are *not* the father *not* the father!
You are *not* the father *not* the father!

You are *not* the father *not* the father!
You are *not* the father *not* the father!
You are *not* the father *not* the father!
You are *not* the father *not* the father!

You are *not* the father *not* the father!

You are *not* the father *not* the father!

Are you?

Piss lattes in the tree corner.

Throw up wingless angles. It's okay?

Clouds nimbus. Everybody's looking.

Just standing there: everybody watches the screams.

:: flutes : bagpipes, trumpets : bassoons, sparrows : grackles ::

Flip blue wide-brim outside-out like father, like —

Do you think your hat is on the wrong way maybe?

$$I(\nu, T) = \frac{2h\nu^3}{c^2} \cdot \frac{1}{e^{\frac{h\nu}{kT}} - 1}$$

Where you are is gonna be really unsafe soon.

Keyon Gaskin

CORONAGRAPHY

John Henry crosses the threshold —

Everyone up here called me crazy but
I couldn't do nothing but what seemed right.
Crazy to fight — maybe — maybe crazy
enough to win. Every day I crouch down

into that bend I know I might not creep
out again. Tunnels eat men like penance —
like payment for letting us through   I knew
my life would be short would be fast but each

shaft of light that snuck through the cracks I smacked
in them walls kept me going and led me

right back — *swinging* — up this yap and folks thought
I was crazy try'n'a dream us up a
future even if I couldn't see it
through all that dust   those sudden

                                        shouts and screams.

Polly Ann tastes victory —

Through all that dust   through sudden shouts and screams
them men slapped their backsides and busted their seams

jumping and hollering — *yeah yeah* — skirts kicked
high — *yeah yeah* — necks dipped low — *yeah yeah* — steam shot

straight to the sky. It knocked and it choked as
that engine died down to a whimper could

barely be heard through the change that crowed and
cursed changing hands over wagers that pit

a week's wages against whoever they
thought could best this mountain. Only fools bet

money on that man's machine and I knew
them fools needed to get on 'way from me

when everyone hollered quick and jumped back
when I watched him crack like steel-bitten stone.

John Henry gets his big break —

When my last steel bit cracked stone I watched her
run through the crowd to come celebrate. I

opened my mouth to say — *I beat him* — but
I stopped when the look in her eyes fell back

when it all went black   when I choked and spat
slumped across her lap and begged for water

and if I spoke I said — *baby we won* —
if I could I said — *these machines can't run*

us down and out from all we built broke and
spiked day after night — baby we did it —

I tried to cup her face in my hands but
the tunnel's maw gaped bright white and her eyes

went sloe and if I spoke I said — *Polly*
baby
    are you here
                in this pitch black mouth?

Haunting Polly Ann —

        baby — are you here in this black pitch mouth
        cause I'm here — *swinging* — just like I said I
        would be — *swinging* — and I won't never leave

shhhh — you heard? they said that howl belonged to
some old wolf-ghost dead about ten years now

        won't never leave here — *swinging* — I'll just wait
        and watch as you push through — *swinging* — maybe
        you can help me too —

they say ain't no way outta here but through
so I'm just — *swinging* — got no time for no

                              — light me a candle

kinda mood when I gotta strike fire-bolt
to this same slate — *swinging* — earn us our food

for tomorrow and tomorrow and — *shhhh* —
I can tell my future too. Wan' hear it?

Polly Ann haunts back —

I can tell our futures too. Listen here —

we weren't born to cry — I swear — but we'll still
stand hungry   near dead   while the man says

— *lift and drop* — *lift and drop* — and baby if
it feels like shaking and sounds like screams — it ain't.

We'll steal away stone quick from the sticks to
wherever it is we're meant for. We'll swing

too low — bear too much too long — let loose them
germs blowing past like we ain't here   living.

Who we gon' be?
                      We gon' choke or bust yoke?

Everyone'll call us crazy but we'll
fly through all their dusty screams and we'll drill

our last bits. They'll watch but they still won't see —
not us baby —
                      climbing this pitch
                                        black mouth.

$$I(\nu, T) = \frac{2h\nu^3}{c^2} \cdot \frac{1}{e^{\frac{h\nu}{kT}} - 1}$$

Ten minutes before you're dead, you're alive.

Gwendolyn Brooks

Zeroth law

When leaning on the backyard beam
beneath a full wolf moon and my slippers
shiver under my nightdress as I happen
upon a reason for waking   call it a snowflake

a belly-flop blue jay or even my own small toe
peeking through a not-yet hole as it fissures into
my slipper's future and I'm not out for a jog or
to find a misplaced piece of scoundrel lover

but to marry my morning coffee to
an old cigarette to the new blue-gray light
of an icy pacific year in mid-set

See how they swinghold hands and raise the sun?
    Hey, you! Bluebird! Whatever will we do
        — *exhale* — with all of these merciful gifts?

At Harlem Hospital across the street from the Schomburg the only thing to eat is a Big Mac

-after Z.S.

Still, somehow we are
carousel. We spin bodies
to the wall and back.

We are woman and
man and man. We
are surgeon and

operation. We are
everybody we love.
We are inside them.

We are inside and we
are laughing. We are
man and we will die too.

We know that much.
We are our own
shadow. We are want

of touch. We are woman
and man and man don't look.
We are curvature — look!

We are train.
We are star.
We are big

tiny spiders. We are
crawling. We are biting.
We are hungry. We are

a stopped carousel. We are
bodies dropped to the floor.
We are shaking. We are our own.

Still, somehow, we are
laughter. We are the doorway out.
We are (again) the doorway in.

Right and title

Know all   that I   of
                    have this day sold
my negro   for the sum of
           payment of which I hereby acknowledge
        made to me, that is to say, by payment to
             the sum of   in satisfaction of a debt
owed   and the sum of   to
in past payment of a debt I owe   The right and title
to   said negro   I hereby warrant   will
forever defend
           Witness my hand   seal this

A small matter of engineering

The old water tower once stored
every drop we lived on. Its walls

dark capped bricked beige as
supermarket pantyhose still rise

erect astride the main drag
where our road splits between

opposing camps. On this side
everything gone as long as anyone

remembers and winter still cold
as it's ever been. On the other side?

Listen. You've always had the broadest
swath of the river, friend. Thing is: we're

still here. Whatever else you've got left —
well — let us stay parched. G'head, I dare you:

Acknowledgements

Deep thanks to the editors of the following transports in which some of these theories originally appeared, often in different form:

- "Field theories," "You don't have to pump the breaks, you just gotta keep your eyes on the road," "Sometimes in a body," and "Notions of temperature," *Drunken Boat*
- "Synchronous rotation," *Portland Monthly*
- "Blackbody curve," "Consequences of the laws of thermodynamics," and "Carnot cycle," *Poetry Magazine*
- "Blackbody curve," *Bettering American Poetry*
- "Paleontology," "Third law," *The Offing Magazine*
- "A small matter of engineering," *Ecotone: Reimagining Place*
- "Zeroth law," *World Literature Today*
- "When I say radiation I mean light that you cannot contain," *Tuesday; An Art Project*
- "Upon such rocks," *Bone Bouquet*
- "Ha ha ha niggers are the worst," *Nepantla Journal*
- "We call it dark matter because it doesn't interact with light," "Transitive relations," *The Normal School*
- "Right and title," *Transition: The Magazine of Africa and the Diaspora*
- "Relations between planets and stars," *Michigan Quarterly Review*
- "Coronagraphy," *Poet Lore*
- "Sore broken in the space of dragons," and "Law of total probability," *Foglifter*
- "Planck's constant," *Crab Orchard Review*
- "Synchronous rotation," "Perform since you must perform," "Radio ∴ Wave," *Hubbub*

- "Manistee light," *Taos Journal of Poetry & Art*
- "Dag! We ain't even in Detroit yet? Sheeeit. Stop here and lemme get me some chicken," *CURA: A Literary Magazine of Art and Action*
- "Ground state," *Rumpus Original Poetry Anthology*
- "Manistee light," *Cascadia Review*
- "General relativities," "Particle $\therefore$ Wave," *Eleven Eleven Journal of Literature & Art*
- "Universe as an infant, fatter than expected and kind of lumpy," *The Encyclopedia Project, Vol. 3, L-Z*

NIGHTBOAT BOOKS

Nightboat Books, a nonprofit organization, seeks to develop audiences for writers whose work resists convention and transcends boundaries. We publish books rich with poignancy, intelligence, and risk. Please visit our website, www.nightboat.org, to learn about our titles and how you can support our future publications.

The following individuals have supported the publication of this book. We thank them for their generosity and commitment to the mission of Nightboat Books:

Elizabeth Motika
Benjamin Taylor

In addition, this book has been made possible, in part, by grants from The National Endowment for the Arts and The New York State Council on the Arts Literature Program.